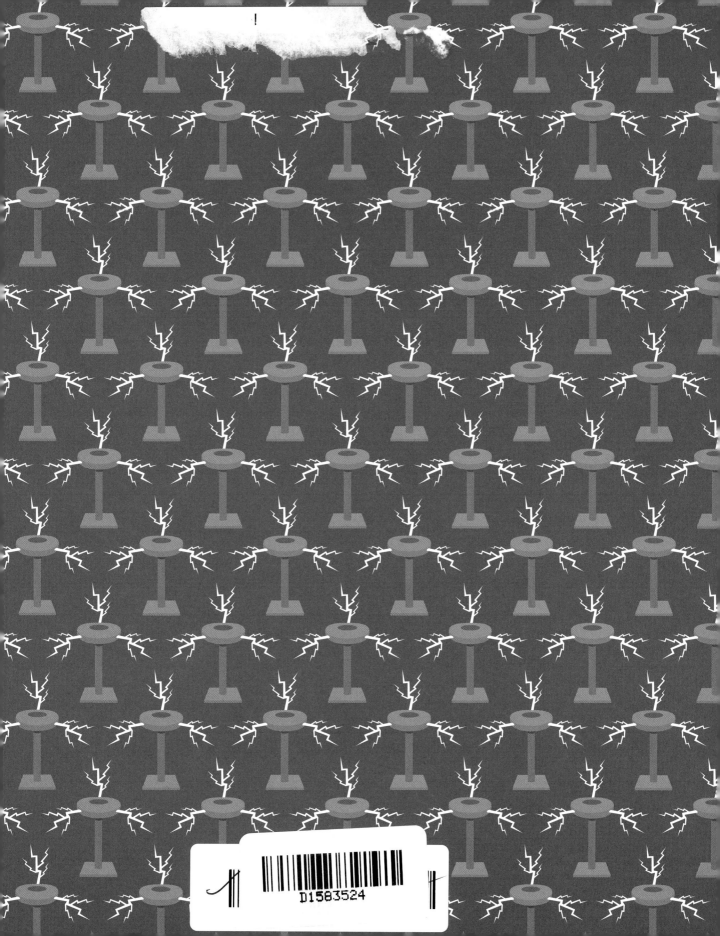

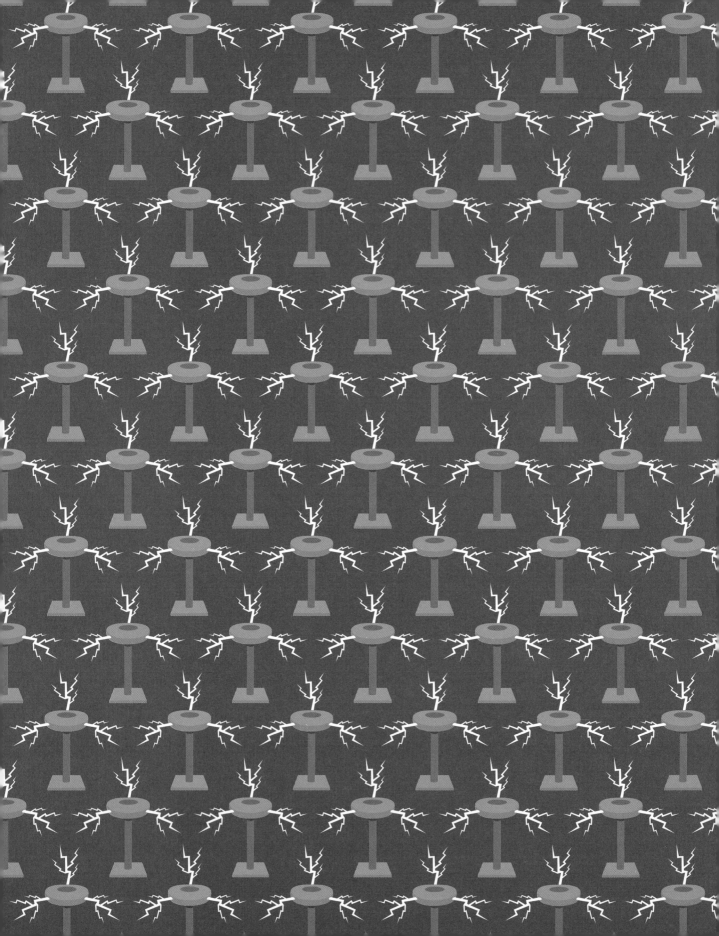

NIKOLA TESLA

GREAT LIVES IN GRAPHICS

Button
BOOKS

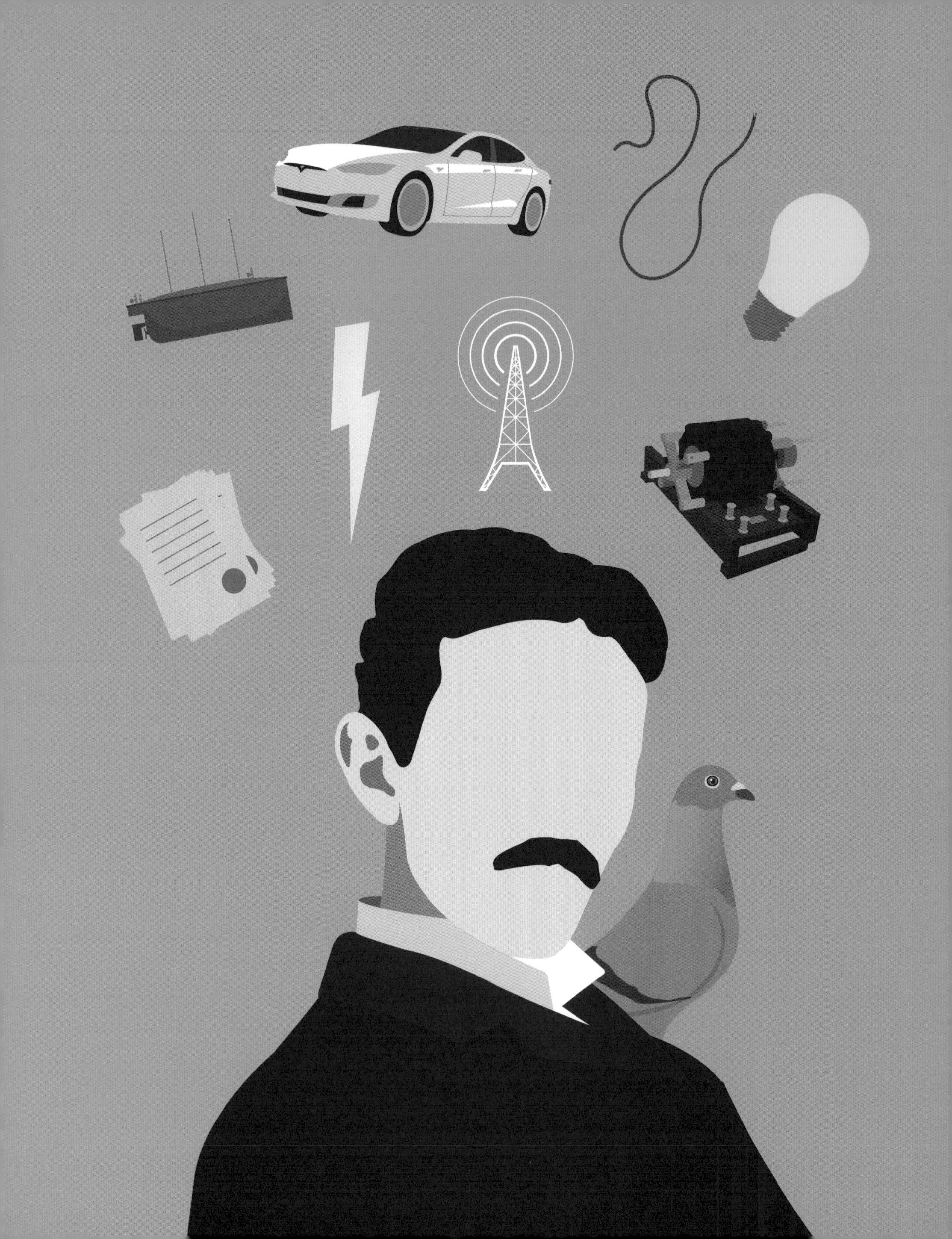

Nikola Tesla was a brilliant engineer who made it possible for us to use electricity in the way we do today. Every time you turn on a light, the technology used can be traced back to Nikola. Able to use his imagination to create crystal-clear pictures of his inventions in his head, his work led to advances in lighting, X-rays, radar, robotics, and more. And yet he hasn't always received the recognition he deserves.

Some people will tell you that is because his rival, Thomas Edison, took all the glory. Others might say Nikola's ideas were stolen by inventors like Guglielmo Marconi. But the truth isn't that simple. Nikola was a visionary whose electrical innovations transformed America and the rest of the world, but he also got things wrong and made mistakes. He was a genius whose ideas were often far ahead of his time, but he also made some grand claims that have never been proven. His quirks and eccentricities are what make him so fascinating. Welcome to the weird and wonderful world of Nikola Tesla…

NIKOLA'S WORLD

1877 Billy the Kid kills first victim

1875
Nikola goes to technical college in Austria

1879
Thomas Edison patents first light bulb

1856
Nikola is born on July 10 in Smiljan, Austrian Empire (now part of Croatia)

1873
Blue jeans patented

1882
Nikola has vision of AC motor. Moves to Paris

1859
Charles Darwin publishes *On the Origin of Species*

1870
Nikola goes to school in Karlovac

1883
Krakatoa volcano erupts

1861 American Civil War begins

28	52
Ni	**Te**
Nickel	Tellurium

1869
Russian scientist Dmitri Mendeleev creates Periodic Table

1884
Nikola moves to New York

1863 Nikola's brother Dane dies

1889
Eiffel Tower opens in Paris

1865 *Alice's Adventures in Wonderland* published

1891
Nikola invents Tesla coil. Becomes US citizen

1918
WWI ends

1923
Walt Disney company founded

1892
First game of basketball played in US

1916
Receives Edison Medal

1927
First non-stop flight across the Atlantic Ocean

1931
Features on cover of *Time* magazine

TIME
The Weekly Newsmagazine

NIKOLA TESLA

1895
Nikola's New York laboratory is destroyed by fire

1914
WWI begins

1912
Titanic sinks

1934
Talks about Teleforce

1901
Marconi transmits letter "S" across Atlantic Ocean

1905
Albert Einstein publishes Theory of Relativity

1939
WWII begins

1943
Dies in New York on January 7, aged 86. US Supreme Court rules that Nikola, not Marconi, was true inventor of radio

R.I.P.
JANUARY 7
1943
(age 86)

1904
Marconi awarded US patent for radio

BRIGHT SPARK

Legend has it Nikola was born on the stroke of midnight in the middle of a summer storm. As bolts of lightning lit up the sky, the midwife turned to Nikola's mother and whispered, "He'll be a child of the storm." "No," Nikola's mother replied, "of light."

NIKOLA GREW UP on a farm in the small village of Smiljan, in the Austro-Hungarian province of Lika (now part of Croatia), with his three sisters–Angelina, Milka, and Marica–and his older brother Dane.

NIKOLA'S DAD, MILUTIN, was a Serbian priest at the village church and he hoped Nikola would follow in his footsteps one day.

Milutin

Angelina Milka Marica

3x 👩
1x 👨

Đuka

NIKOLA'S MOM, ĐUKA, ran the farm. Having never been to school (when she was little her own mother lost her eyesight and Đuka stayed home to help), Đuka couldn't read or write. Despite this, she had an **INCREDIBLE MEMORY** and was a **BRILLIANT INVENTOR**, creating tools such as a mechanical egg beater to use on the farm.

One of Nikola's first inventions was an insect-powered propeller. He made blades from thin sticks and glued bugs to them, hoping that when they beat their wings the propeller would turn. It did! *

*Please, kids, don't try this at home.

THE FAMILY CAT, MACAK,

was Nikola's closest companion. While stroking its back one evening he was amazed to see sparks. "It's electricity," his dad told him, "the same thing you see through trees in a storm." Nikola's imagination was set alight. "Is nature a gigantic cat?" he thought. "If so, who strokes its back?"

Curious and a little reckless, Nikola got himself into all sorts of scrapes.

Around five years old, he jumped from the roof of the barn with an umbrella, convinced he could fly. Another time he nearly died after falling into a vat of hot milk!

AGE 5

THUNDER CRASH

Thunder is one of nature's loudest sounds–thunderclaps can reach 120 decibels!

dB	Source
190	VOLCANIC ERUPTION
180	ROCKET LAUNCH
160	SHOTGUN BLAST
140	JET PLANE TAKEOFF
130	PAIN THRESHOLD
120	LOUD THUNDER, ROCK CONCERT
110	CHAINSAW, JET SKI
100	SYMPHONY ORCHESTRA
90	LAWN MOWER

Sounds above 85dB can be harmful the longer you're exposed to them

dB	Source
85	LOUD TRAFFIC, NOISY RESTAURANT
70	VACUUM CLEANER, WASHING MACHINE
60	NORMAL CONVERSATION
40	QUIET OFFICE, AVERAGE HOME
25	WHISPER
10	BREATHING

AGE 6 Nikola's dad gets a new job and they move to Gospić. It's only a few miles from Smiljan, but Nikola thinks the town is too busy and misses the countryside.

AGE 7 Nikola's older brother Dane falls from a horse and dies. Nikola sees the accident happen and is deeply affected. He worries he'll never fill his brother's shoes.

AGE 10 At school Nikola is so good at mental math his teachers think he's cheating.

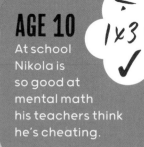

BELGIUM

GERMANY

FRANCE   PARIS

KARLOVAC

SMILJAN

GOSPIĆ

CULTURE SHOCK

From a young age, Nikola showed traits of genius. Taught at some of the finest schools in Europe, he had a flair for spotting more efficient ways of doing things and by age 19 was pointing out design flaws in the electrical motors demonstrated by his professors.

ITALY

AGE 25 Moves to Paris, joins the Continental Edison Company as an electrical engineer.

AGE 23 Studies briefly in Prague, then moves to Budapest. Walking through a park he has a vision of a new kind of electrical motor and draws it in the dirt with a stick.

AGE 22 The police find Nikola and send him home to Gospić, but a month later his dad dies. Nikola is devastated.

DAD

AGE 14 Goes to school in Karlovac. Stays with his aunt and uncle, an "old war-horse" who'd fought in many battles. They're strict and feed Nikola "like a canary bird."

AGE 15 Built on the banks of four rivers, Karlovac is infested with mosquitoes. Nikola catches malaria and gets a fever. He opens a book about Niagara Falls and imagines the waters turning a gigantic wheel, which in turn powers a city. Nothing like it had ever been seen before. He tells his uncle that one day he will go to America and make it happen!

MALARIA

AGE 17 Graduates with honors. Returns home to Gospić, catches cholera, and is bedridden for nine months. Worried Nikola may die, his dad promises he can forget priesthood and study engineering if he lives.

CHOLERA

PRAGUE

CZECH REPUBLIC

POLAND

SLOVAKIA

UKRAINE

AUSTRIA

BUDAPEST

HUNGARY

GRAZ

MARIBOR

ROMANIA

AGE 18 Nikola's dad sends him to a village in the mountains to build up his strength and avoid being drafted by the army.

SLOVENIA

CROATIA

SERBIA

BOSNIA & HERZEGOVINA

AGE 21 Starts gambling, loses his tuition money, and drops out of university. Too ashamed to tell his dad the truth, Nikola goes into hiding in Maribor, Slovenia.

AGE 19 Wins scholarship to study at Graz Polytechnic in Austria. Works from 3am to 11pm every day and aces his exams, but Nikola's teachers warn him he's working too hard.

3AM — 11PM

MACEDONIA

MIND'S EYE

Nikola could visualize objects in his head with incredible clarity, picturing them as vividly as the real thing. He used this skill to "see" his inventions before trying to create them. Today scientists call this ability hyperphantasia, but they still don't fully understand it.

How clearly do you experience images in your mind's eye **?**

TASTE

Picture a pizza on a plate

- Can you taste it? Is it salty?
- Which taste stands out more, tomato or cheese?
- Imagine adding onion and olives. Can you taste the difference between them?
- What flavor is missing that would make it taste more delicious?

SEE

Picture a ball on the grass

- Can you see what color it is?
- Is there a pattern?
- Is it smooth and shiny, or are there bumps or ridges on its surface?
- How much of the ball is sitting in the grass?
- Can you easily zoom in on the ball, and rotate it?

HEAR

Imagine you're listening to a favorite song

- Can you hear the different instruments?
- How clear are the vocals?
- Can you make out the words?
- Can you change the tempo—slow the song down and speed it back up?
- What about making the singer sound high-pitched, like they've breathed in helium?

DID YOU KNOW?

NIKOLA HAD A
PHOTOGRAPHIC MEMORY

SPOKE 8 LANGUAGES

ENGLISH | HUNGARIAN

ITALIAN | LATIN | SERBO-CROATIAN | FRENCH | GERMAN | CZECH

TOUCH

Picture your hand and a teddy bear in front of you

- Can you reach out your hand and touch the bear?
- Does it feel soft?
- Can you pick the bear up?
- Is it light or heavy?
- Can you snap your fingers? Do you feel your fingers touch?

SMELL

Imagine a pot of lavender

- Can you smell it?
- Is the smell strong or faint?
- Can you tell it's lavender?
- Can you make it smell like something else, a favorite food maybe?
- What about mixing smells? Lavender, perfume, stinky cheese?

—''—

During my boyhood I had suffered from a peculiar affliction due to the appearance of images, which were often accompanied by strong flashes of light. When a word was spoken, the image of the object designated would present itself so vividly to my vision that I could not tell whether what I saw was real or not ... Even though I reached out and passed my hand through it, the image would remain fixed in space

NIKOLA TESLA

—''—

Electric DREAMS

Nikola was obsessed with electricity from a young age. But what is it exactly and how does it work?

ATOMS

EVERYTHING YOU CAN SEE–your hand, the ground, the trees, the sky, and the buildings–is made of atoms. **ATOMS ARE SUPER TINY**, but to find out how electricity works, we have to go even smaller, to what atoms are made of.

What is ELECTRICITY?

When we say that a material is electric, we mean that it has an **electric charge**. To explain what that is, first we need to zoom in a little...

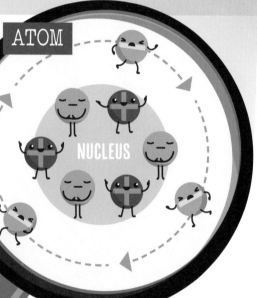
ATOM

NUCLEUS

ATOMS contain three different particles

ELECTRONS

- Smallest and lightest particles
- NEGATIVE ⊖ charge
- Move fast around the atom's nucleus

PROTONS

- Larger and heavier particles
- POSITIVE ⊕ charge
- Stay in the center (nucleus)

NEUTRONS

- Larger and heavier particles
- No charge
- Stay in the center (nucleus)

ELECTRIC CHARGE

Opposite charges attract one another, while charges that are the same repel each other.

OPPOSITES ATTRACT

LIKES REPEL

Usually there are the same number of positive protons and negative electrons in an atom, so they balance each other out.

But sometimes if you push an atom with an outside negative or positive charge, you can force one of the electrons to jump off the atom and become free!

BOLT FROM THE BLUE

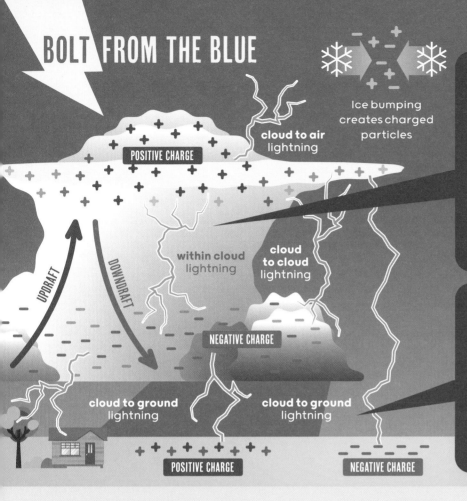

Ice bumping creates charged particles

cloud to air lightning

POSITIVE CHARGE

UPDRAFT

DOWNDRAFT

within cloud lightning

cloud to cloud lightning

NEGATIVE CHARGE

cloud to ground lightning

cloud to ground lightning

POSITIVE CHARGE

NEGATIVE CHARGE

Lightning is an electric current. During a storm, thunderclouds fill up with tiny bits of ice that move around and bump into each other, creating negative and positively charged particles. Most of the positively charged particles rise to the top of the cloud, while the negatively charged particles sit at the bottom. When there are enough, a giant spark occurs between the two–this is lightning!

Most lightning happens inside a cloud, but sometimes positively charged particles build up on the ground beneath the cloud. They group together around anything that sticks up–trees, spires, or even people. When the two connect, negative charges race toward the ground and we see a flash of lightning.

An atom with an electron removed or an electron added is **ELECTRICALLY CHARGED**.

ELECTRIC CURRENT

Now imagine a copper wire–the wire is filled with millions of copper atoms.

There's a **free electron** floating in space between atoms. Suddenly it bumps into a copper atom and latches onto it. As it does so, its **negative charge** pushes another electron free.

This new floating electron does the same thing, and before you know it you have a chain of electrons jumping from one atom to the next. This is what we call an **electric current**.

Lightning is so hot it can heat the air around it to

54,000°F
(30,000°C)

5x hotter than the sun's surface!

Lightning's heat causes the air around it to vibrate, creating **THUNDER**

Around
24,000 PEOPLE
are killed by lightning every year!

A flow of electrons from atom to atom is an electric current. Another name for that is **ELECTRICITY**

 bump bump bump

FREE ELECTRON

Nikola's sickly childhood gave him a lifelong fear of germs and he always wore gloves, even in summer! He bought them by the bucketload, all in the same gray suede.
But that wasn't his only eccentricity...

Stranger things

Nikola was OBSESSED WITH THE NUMBER 3

HE WALKED around buildings **THREE TIMES** before entering.

He used **18 NAPKINS** while eating (because 18 is divisible by three!).

He regularly **SWAM 33 LAPS** at his local pool, insisting on starting over if he lost count.

He lived the last 10 years of his life in room number **3327** on the **33RD FLOOR** of the New Yorker Hotel.

3327

Nikola was a famous night owl. He often worked day and night without stopping, averaging only:

2 HOURS SLEEP A NIGHT

He couldn't stand the sight of pearl earrings and refused to speak to any woman who wore them!

Nikola couldn't enjoy food or drink unless he'd worked out its volume first.

Nikola often counted his steps when walking.

HE DIDN'T LIKE TOUCHING HAIR OR SHAKING HANDS
probably from fear of germs.

He curled the toes on each of his feet

100 TIMES EVERY NIGHT
saying it stimulated his brain cells.

WHAT ARE YOU AFRAID OF?

Almost everyone is afraid of something, but sometimes fears become stronger than usual and turn into phobias. Here are a few less well-known ones...

MACROPHOBIA
The fear of long waits.

OMPHALOPHOBIA
The fear of belly buttons.

KATHISOPHOBIA
The fear of sitting down.

NOMOPHOBIA
The fear of not having access to your phone.

DENDROPHOBIA
The fear of trees.

DEXTROPHOBIA
The fear of having objects on your right.

GENUPHOBIA
The fear of knees.

SYNGENESOPHOBIA
The fear of relatives.

Aged 28 Nikola left Paris for New York to work for the great Thomas Edison. Both inventors had a talent for improving existing technologies, but when it came to money they didn't see eye to eye. Within a year, Nikola had struck out on his own and the two giants of electrical engineering became bitter rivals.

NIKOLA
TESLA

A.K.A. THE WIZARD OF THE WEST

B.F.F.
MARK TWAIN

WORK METHOD

TECHNICAL THEORY

No. OF PATENTS

300+

FAMOUS INVENTIONS

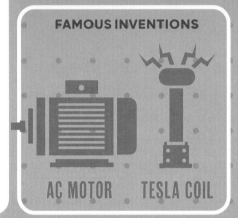

AC MOTOR   TESLA COIL

86

1943

WIVES

0

CHILDREN

0

POSSIBLE CONDITION

OCD

SLEEP

2 HRS

HEIGHT

6 ft 2 in
(1.88m)

LIFESPAN

1856

66 Be alone, that is the secret of invention; be alone, that is when ideas are born 99

Died
IN DEBT

SMILJAN, AUSTRO-HUNGARIAN EMPIRE

THOMAS EDISON

A.K.A. THE WIZARD OF MENLO PARK

Averaged across his adult life, Edison patented something roughly

EVERY **11** DAYS

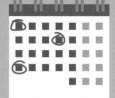

LIFESPAN

84

1931

1847

FAMOUS INVENTIONS

LIGHT BULB   PHONOGRAPH

WORK METHOD

TRIAL & ERROR

No. OF PATENTS

1,093

B.F.F. HENRY FORD

CHILDREN

5

WIVES

2

POSSIBLE CONDITION

DYS-LEXIA

SLEEP

3-4HRS

HEIGHT

5 ft 10 in
(1.78m)

MILAN, OHIO, USA

Fortune **$12MILLION**

" Genius is 1% inspiration and 99% perspiration "

AC/DC

WAR OF THE CURRENTS

Nikola and Thomas Edison went to war over which electricity system would be best for delivering power to people's homes and businesses–alternating current (AC) or direct current (DC). Edison championed DC and Nikola favored AC. Who do you think won?

Edison patented the first practical light bulb in 1879.

He began building a system to get electricity to people's homes so they could use his invention.

ELECTRICITY FLOWS STEADILY IN ONE DIRECTION.

DC

Edison used DC motors because they were easy to design.

ELECTRICITY FLOWS BACK AND FORTH CONSTANTLY.

AC

Nikola tried to interest Edison in his AC motor invention, but Edison said AC had...

When Nikola saw a DC motor being demonstrated at university, he knew there were problems with it and began thinking of a solution.

Walking in a park with a friend Nikola had a vision of how an AC motor could work.

...NO FUTURE!

DID YOU KNOW?

To make ends meet after he quit his job with Edison, Nikola worked as a

DITCH DIGGER FOR 2 YEARS **EARNING JUST** **$2 PER DAY**

USES

Solar panels

Batteries

LEDs

Nikola quit his job with Edison and joined forces with an entrepreneur named George Westinghouse. Together they developed working AC motors.

In 1893, Nikola and Westinghouse showcased their AC motors to the world in a dazzling display.

By 1887, Edison had built

121 DC POWER STATIONS

all across America.

Edison was sure that DC was best. When Nikola's AC motors started getting attention, he was worried. He told everyone that AC was dangerous and tried to prove it by electrocuting an elephant named Topsy with a 6,600-volt AC charge! Poor Topsy died instantly.

DC can't travel very far before it loses energy. This meant power stations had to be built close to the homes they were supplying electricity to, and lots of them were needed.

★★★★★
WINNER

Nikola's AC system could send electricity long distances safely and supply thousands of homes with just one large power plant.

Soon after, they built a hydroelectric power plant at Niagara Falls powered by AC generators. It sent electricity all the way to Buffalo in New York, 26 miles away. Nikola had solved the problem of how to send power safely and efficiently to homes, shops, and factories. AC had won the war of the currents!

Car motors

Appliances

Household supply

RADIO GO-GO

Nikola was convinced electricity could be beamed wirelessly around the world, instantly and for free. In the midst of his wireless work he stumbled across numerous new technologies—radio, X-rays, and neon light. But his dream of free energy remained just out of reach...

1891

Nikola patented a powerful coil capable of shooting bolts of electricity, leading to new forms of light like neon and fluorescent and eventually X-rays. His "Tesla coil" could also send radio signals, but he decided it was too slow for long-distance communication.

1900

Excited by his success in the lab, Nikola returned to New York with hopes of constructing an enormous tower, which would pump waves of current through the Earth, to be picked up by special stations all over the globe. Almost broke, he borrowed money and began building a year later.

1899

Nikola believed he could use the Earth itself as a giant conductor to produce never-ending amounts of energy. He built a laboratory in Colorado Springs with a 49 ft (15m)-wide Tesla coil, the largest ever created. It shot out 135 ft-long lightning bolts and the thunder generated could be heard 15 miles (25km) away!

135 ft (41m) LONG

1898

Radio was the hot new topic in science circles and Nikola wowed astonished crowds at New York's Madison Square Garden with his demonstration of a radio-controlled boat.

Today there's a Tesla coil in almost every broadcasting antenna and car ignition system.

MARS ATTACKS

One day Nikola's equipment at Colorado Springs picked up a series of beeps. Mystified as to their origin, he concluded they might be from Mars!

GRANDMASTER FLASH!

Nikola's Tesla coil at Colorado Springs generated millions of volts, producing gigantic artificial lightning bolts up to

135 FT (41M) LONG!

Legend has it people walking past saw sparks darting between their feet and the ground.

Light bulbs close by glowed even when switched off.

Nikola noted horses in a nearby field jumping to escape the shocks surging through their metal shoes.

Butterflies fluttering in the air outside were said to be electrified, their wings surrounded by gleaming blue halos.

1901

The world was racing to send radio signals long distances and Nikola promised the bank his Wardenclyffe tower would be the first to do it. But after Italian physicist Guglielmo Marconi broadcast the first radio signal across the Atlantic Ocean, Nikola's cash dried up.

1906

Now Nikola's dreams lay in tatters. Research by other scientists showed his ideas were flawed, but Nikola refused to accept it. The costs of the tower ballooned as he desperately tried to make it work. Finally, up to his eyes in debt, the tower was demolished in 1917 and sold as scrap.

COLORADO SPRINGS

WARDENCLYFFE

THE GREATEST
SHOWMAN

Nikola had a flair for both science and showmanship. A master of electricity at a time when electricity was transforming the world, he quickly earned a reputation for his dazzling experiments.

One of Nikola's first great demonstrations was his Egg of Columbus. Inspired by the story that Italian navigator Columbus won over Queen Isabella of Spain by promising to balance an egg on its end (by cracking it), Nikola used a rotating magnetic field to spin a copper egg on its point!

EGG of COLUMBUS

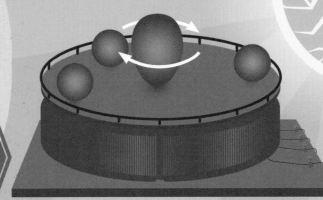

To show a disbelieving public how safe AC current was, Nikola stood on a stage and allowed

250,000 VOLT SHOCKS

to course across his body!

BODY SHOCK

WEIRD SCIENCE

When friends like author Mark Twain showed up at his lab, Nikola would entertain them with electrical trickery. One story goes that when Mark complained of constipation, Nikola directed him to stand on his oscillator. He flipped a switch and two minutes later Mark was rushing to the toilet!

FAMOUS
MARK TWAIN
AUTHOR

One day Nikola attached an oscillator to an iron pillar in his New York lab.

THE BUILDING SHOOK, WINDOWS BROKE & VIBRATIONS WERE FELT MILES AWAY

Two police officers sent to investigate the earthquake arrived to find Nikola trying to shut down the oscillator with a sledgehammer. Later he told reporters he had a pocket-sized version that could bring down the Brooklyn Bridge!

DOUBLE VISION

To amaze the public (and keep money coming in from his investors) Nikola published miraculous photos of himself sitting beneath a Tesla coil at Colorado Springs—he used a double exposure to create the images.

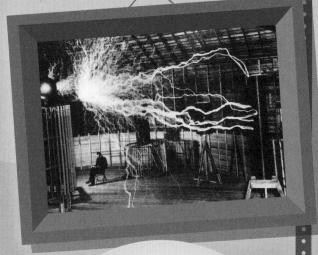

LET THERE BE LIGHT

Nikola helped illuminate the Chicago World Fair—an exhibition designed to showcase the world's achievements—with 200,000 electric lamps, more than could be found in the entire city of Chicago!

TIME LORD

Whenever you power up your computer, turn on a light, or put food in the oven, the technology used can be traced back to Nikola. But his genius wasn't limited to electricity. He started dozens of projects that were decades ahead of their time, only to drop them to focus on his dream of wireless power.

1893
Nikola's use of phosphorescent lamps

1930s
Public use

1898
Nikola's radio-controlled boat

1940s
Available to the public

1899
Nikola's use of wireless electricity

1960s
First long-distance wireles transfer (using microwave

1902 Nikola's proposal for an instant communication handheld device

1917
Nikola's concept for radar

1930s
Radar developed

1921
Nikola's design for a helicopter-plane

1950s
US military build similar aircraft

1890 1900 1910 1920 1930 1940 1950 1960 1970 1980

DID YOU KNOW?

A patent registers your invention and allows you to take legal action against anyone who uses, makes, or sells the same thing without your permission.

FATHER OF INVENTION?

Japanese inventor Yoshiro Nakamatsu (aka Dr. NakaMats) has **3,500+ PATENTS!**

3x the number of Thomas Edison in the US. Some of his inventions include:

- The floppy disk
- A toilet seat-lifter
- A wig with a built-in sword
- A musical golf putter
- Jumping shoes

—❝—

I do not think there is any thrill that can go through the human heart like that felt by the inventor as he sees some creation of the brain unfolding to success... such emotions make a man forget food, sleep, friends, love, everything

NIKOLA TESLA

—❞—

2000s
Smartphone technology

2000   2010   2020

DEATH RAY

In later years, Nikola moved from hotel to hotel to escape mounting bills. Lacking the money to pay his debt at the Hotel Governor Clinton, instead he offered them the rights to one of his most astonishing inventions: a "death beam." When the hotel agreed, he gave them a mysterious wooden box, warning them it was so deadly it could explode if opened incorrectly!

It could kill an army of

1 MILLION SOLDIERS

Daily Post

Tesla's DEATH RAY

Nikola called it a **TELEFORCE**

but the press nicknamed it the **DEATH RAY**

WOULD IT WORK?

Like many of Nikola's later inventions, the particle beam weapon was never built, but he did produce detailed plans.

It would bring down a fleet of

10,000
ENEMY AIRCRAFT

✈ = 100 AIRCRAFT

BOX OF TRICKS

After Nikola's death, the Hotel Governor Clinton told the government about the box in their vault and scientist John G. Trump (Donald Trump's uncle) was sent to assess it. Worried the package had been booby-trapped, John said a short prayer before gathering his courage and tearing it open. Inside was nothing but a few old electrical parts. Nikola had fooled them all!

BOOBY TRAP?

Nikola claimed his new weapon would

SHOOT A JET OF
METAL
AT
PARTICLES

200,000
MILES PER HOUR
(434,523 km/h)

Feathered FRIENDS

Nikola loved pigeons. For 30 years he fed them in parks across New York and took sick ones home to his hotel room to nurse back to health. His favorite was a special white female with light gray wing tips: "I loved that pigeon as a man loves a woman," he said, "and she loved me."

Love bird

Nikola said he had only to think of the white pigeon and call her and she would show up.

PARK LIFE

Alone in a park, often after midnight, Nikola would blow a bird whistle and pigeons would flock to him. They perched on his head, arms, and shoulders and ate seeds from his hands.

$2,000
The amount Nikola spent on caring for the white pigeon when it broke a wing and leg. He even made a special device to support it.

IN TODAY'S MONEY
that would be around
$30,000!

LIGHTS OUT

One night Nikola's white pigeon flew through an open window into his hotel room. He saw "two powerful beams of light" in the bird's eyes. "Yes, it was a real light, a powerful, dazzling, blinding light, a light more intense than I had ever produced by the most powerful lamps in my laboratory." The pigeon died in his arms and Nikola felt his life's work was finished.

DNA testing has confirmed pigeons are closely related to the extinct dodo bird.

PIGEONS SAVED 1,000s of lives during WWII by delivering messages.

—**"**—

That pigeon was the joy of my life. If she needed me, nothing else mattered. As long as I had her, there was a purpose in my life

NIKOLA TESLA

—**"**—

Pigeons can find their way back to a nest from **1,300 MILES AWAY**

A baby pigeon is called a squab.

PIGEONS HAVE **10,000** FEATHERS

HIDE AND SEEK

When Nikola was due to receive the Edison Medal in 1917 he disappeared from the ceremony and was found feeding pigeons in a park around the corner.

Speed of the fastest racing pigeon

110 MPH (177 km/h)

More than **400 MILLION** pigeons in the world.

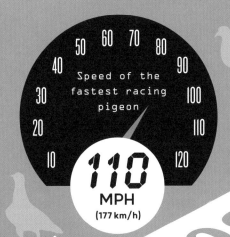

308 species of pigeon and dove.

BRIGHT FUTURE

Nikola died in his sleep at the New Yorker Hotel aged 86. Today, if you type "Tesla" into a search engine, most results refer to Tesla Inc, Elon Musk's revolutionary electric car company. Named for Nikola, in a way it's working toward his dream of transmitting electrical energy around the world, just through battery technology rather than broadcast power.

30 MINUTES

The time taken to charge a Model S at a Tesla Supercharger.

Wheels of fortune

Nikola would have been delighted that, despite using DC batteries, Tesla cars all have AC motors.

$40,000

Starting cost of a Model 3.

5¢
Average cost per mile for a Model 3 – a quarter of the cost of gasoline.

£3
£2
£1

20,000
The number of

TESLA
SUPERCHARGERS
around the world.

2.5 SECONDS
0 — 60
The time taken for the Model S to go from 0 to 60mph in

LUDICROUS MODE

The distance a Model 3 will drive on a full charge:

250 MILES
(402 km)

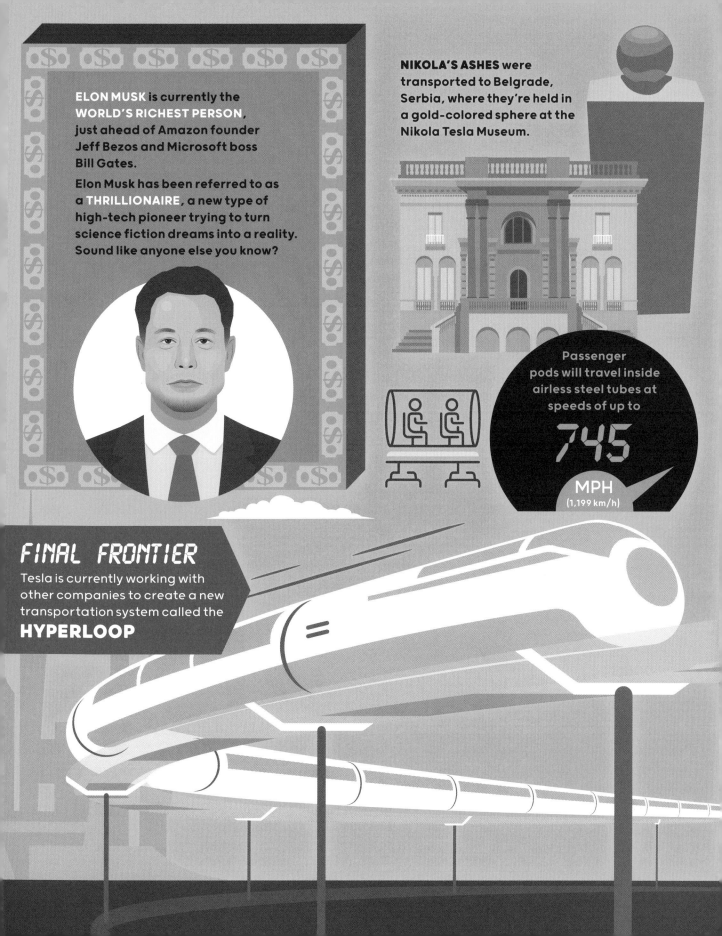

ELON MUSK is currently the **WORLD'S RICHEST PERSON**, just ahead of Amazon founder Jeff Bezos and Microsoft boss Bill Gates.

Elon Musk has been referred to as a **THRILLIONAIRE**, a new type of high-tech pioneer trying to turn science fiction dreams into a reality. Sound like anyone else you know?

NIKOLA'S ASHES were transported to Belgrade, Serbia, where they're held in a gold-colored sphere at the Nikola Tesla Museum.

Passenger pods will travel inside airless steel tubes at speeds of up to

745

MPH
(1,199 km/h)

FINAL FRONTIER
Tesla is currently working with other companies to create a new transportation system called the **HYPERLOOP**

GLOSSARY

ALTERNATING CURRENT
An electric current that reverses its direction many times every second.

ANTENNA
A metal rod or wire used to receive radio signals or transmit them. Sometimes called an aerial.

ATOM
The smallest pieces of matter.

CHOLERA
A disease caused by eating dirty food or drinking dirty water.

CONDUCTOR
A material that an electric charge passes through easily.

DIRECT CURRENT
An electric current that flows in one direction.

ELECTRICITY
The flow of charged particles.

ELECTRIC CHARGE
The property of tiny particles like electrons and protons that makes them stick together to form atoms. There are two types of electric charge: positive and negative.

ELECTRICAL ENGINEER
Engineers who fix, design, and develop devices that use electricity in a helpful way.

ELECTRICAL MOTOR
A device that changes electrical energy into mechanical movement, used in everything from hairdryers to computers to cars.

ELECTRON
A negatively charged particle that spins around an atom's nucleus.

HYDROELECTRIC POWER
Electricity that is made by the movement of water.

HYPERPHANTASIA
The ability to create very clear images in the mind's eye.

MALARIA
A disease that's spread by the bite of mosquitoes.

NEUTRON
A particle with no charge found at the center of an atom.

PATENT
A certificate given to an inventor by the government that says other people can't use or make their invention without permission.

PROTON
A positively charged particle found at the center of an atom.

TESLA COIL
A machine invented by Nikola Tesla that creates lightning bolts.

X-RAY
A type of radiation that passes through things, creating a picture.

Button Books

First published 2021 by Button Books, an imprint of Guild of Master Craftsman Publications Ltd, Castle Place, 166 High Street, Lewes, East Sussex, BN7 1XU, UK. Copyright in the Work © GMC Publications Ltd, 2020. ISBN 978 1 78708 060 7. Distributed by Publishers Group West in the United States. All rights reserved. No part of this publication may be reproduced, stored in a retrieval system, or transmitted in any form or by any means without the prior permission of the publisher and copyright owner. While every effort has been made to obtain permission from the copyright holders for all material used in this book, the publishers will be pleased to hear from anyone who has not been appropriately acknowledged and to make the correction in future reprints. The publishers and authors can accept no legal responsibility for any consequences arising from the application of information, advice, or instructions given in this publication. A catalogue record for this book is available from the British Library. Senior Project Editor: Susie Duff. Design: Tim Lambert, Jo Chapman. Illustrations: Alex Bailey, Matt Carr, Shutterstock. Photography: Alamy. Color origination by GMC Reprographics. Printed and bound in China.